Introduction

Dear Friends,

We are delighted to bring you this second edition of **The Good Heart Cookbook.** Like the popular first edition, this cookbook is full of our most delicious and requested recipes from our retreat center and we are overjoyed to share them with you.

Here Land of Medicine Buddha retreat center, we are propelled by our mission of being "A Center for Healing and Developing a Good Heart." This mission has naturally extended into the area of meals where our chefs strive with love and talent to create and serve abundant vegetarian food options. While the health benefits of a vegetarian diet are well documented, it is the good and kind heart, a truly healthy heart, upon which we place our focus.

In addition to being a vegetarian center, we are a green certified business. We are proud to be part of a growing community of eco responsible businesses. As such we continue to refine our menus to allow us to provide more local, seasonal and organic foods. By following this path, we have found another avenue to extend our spiritual value of non-harming into our business practices.

Finally, when our chefs and kitchen staff are hired, we share with them what we feel is the most important ingredient in all of our meals…love. It is our hope that this love is embraced by you our reader, and shared far and wide.

With heartfelt thanks for all who have visited our center and contributed in so many ways to our success, we humbly give you our second edition of **The Good Heart Cookbook.**

The LMB Cookbook Team:
Denice Macy – Center Director
Venerable Gyalten – Editor
Marti Waite – Editor/Contributing cook
Venerable Anet – Contributing cook
Vimal Dass - Contributing cook
Rachel Enright – Contributing cook
Brian Espanoza – Contributing cook
Eric Oztochane – Contributing cook
Cynthia "Thea" Crossley – Contributing cook
Ruth Nucera – Contributing cook
Karene Percival – Contributing cook
Venerable Driamy – Contributing Author/Editor
Jason "Dorje" Greenburg – Cover and Graphic design
Kyabje Lama Zopa Rinpoche – Momo Recipe/Spiritual Dir. of FPMT

Table of Contents

Menu Options...4
SOUPS:..5
Carrot Red Pepper..6
Coconut Vegetable...7
Corn Chowder...8
Gumbo...9
Hungarian Mushroom..10
Lentil Veggie...11
Minestrone..12
Pea Soup with Tarragon..13
Potato Leek and Arugula..14
Roasted Zucchini...15
Spinach Artichoke...16
Tuscan Bean..17
SALADS & DRESSINGS:..18
Classic Caesar Salad with dressing...19
Cilantro-Lime Vinaigrette..20
Feta Ranch Dressing..21
French Grated Carrot Salad...22
Green Goddess Dressing...23
Honey Mustard Dressing...24
Mayan Dressing...25
Parsley Salad..26
Quinoa Salad..27
Thai Peanut Dressing...28
MAIN DISHES:...29
Black Bean and Zucchini Chilaquiles.......................................30
Coconut Veggie Curry...31
Dahl A La Medicine Buddha...32
Enchiladas..33-34
Magnificent Mushroom Burgers...35
Mushroom Cutlets with Red Pepper Sauce..............................36
Orange Glazed Tempeh..37
Pad Thai..38
Pasta With No-Meat Balls...39
Home Made Marinara Sauce...40
Penne With Gorgonzola and Walnuts.......................................41

Table of Contents

Portabella Tacos..42
Quinoa Frittata with Herbs and Feta...........................43
Ratatouille...44
Shepherd's Pie..45
Spring Thyme Spaghetti..46
Tempeh Stir-fry with Broccoli and Peppers...............47
Three Cheese Baked Polenta.....................................48
Tofu with Aztec Mole..49-50
Vimal's Nut Loaf..51
White Beans and Greens..52
Yams Roasted with Maple Allspice Butter..................53
TIBETAN FOODS:..54
Lama Zopa   Rinpoche's Momo Recipe.................55-56
Momo Hot Sauce..57
Thukpa..58-59
LMB Chai Tea..60
DESSERTS:...61
Chocolate Bark...62
Coconut Custard Pie...63
Coconut Tapioca Pudding...64
Fruit Crisp..65
Karene's   Chocolate Truffles.................................66-67
Strawberry Shortcake...68

EXTRAS:...69
Hummus Wrap...70
Salsa Fresca...71
Savory Pesto Popcorn...72
Spanish Romesco Sauce...73
Tofu Crumble..74

APPENDIX:...
Cooking with Bodhichitta Mindfulness.......................75
Eating with Bodhichitta Mindfulness..........................76
Mahayana Precepts..77
About Land of Medicine Buddha..........................78-79

EDITORS NOTE: Most of these recipes have been adapted from buffet sized servings. You may find further adjustments needed to suit your tastes.

Menu Options

Vegan... Gluten Free... Precept Friendly... Protein Rich...

Here at Land of Medicine Buddha, we know that many of our guests and our staff have specific dietary needs. And we do our best to cater to those needs.

So, we have organized this cookbook to note recipes that are Vegan, Gluten Free, protein rich and friendly for the 8 Mahayana Precepts diet.

Please note that in almost every one of the recipes in this book, substitutions can be made to accommodate your specific needs. Those who are vegan can use non-animal-based ingredients.

Those who are gluten free can substitute wheat flour with rice flour, garbanzo bean flour or whichever suits your taste. Those people who are living in the vows of the 8 Mahayana Precepts can use celery in place of onion and ginger in place of garlic in most cases. There are also vegan egg substitutes that can be used for precept diet.

Upon request from our spiritual director, Kyabje Lama Zopa Rinpoche, we do not serve meat. We know how important it is to get enough protein in our diet. So we do our best to create meals with plenty of tasty protein alternatives.

Feel free to experiment and alter these recipes to fit your dietary preferences and specific tastes.

  Enjoy!

Soups

In the tradition of developing our good heart and being mindful of our health, we usually serve soup at dinner at Land of Medicine Buddha. Eating lightly at dinner is known to be heart-healthy.

We know dinner's almost ready when we walk past the kitchen and smell aroma of the soup simmering on the stove; and what a great way to end the day by sitting down with friends to enjoy it.

From light and refreshing fare like Carrot Pepper soup to rich and hearty like our Lentil Veggie, each of our soups in this cookbook have their own unique tastes that are sure to satisfy.

We've picked the most popular and most requested recipes to use for this cookbook.

VEGAN – GLUTEN FREE – PRECEPT FRIENDLY

Carrot & Red Pepper Soup

Ingredients: Serves 6-8
¼ cup Olive oil
1 1/8 pounds Red bell peppers
1 ½ pounds carrots, thinly sliced
2 stick celery, diced
¼ cup Rice, white or brown, uncooked
½ Tbsp. Salt
¼ cup Parsley, chopped
1/8 cup Dried dill
Pinch of Curry powder
1 ea. Orange, Zest and Juice
Squeeze Lemon Juice
1 quart Vegetable stock
Finely chopped parsley, dill or cilantro – to garnish
Salt and Pepper – to taste

Preparation:
Cut bell peppers into 1 inch pieces. Warm olive oil in a soup pot and add the peppers, carrots, rice, and salt. Cook over medium heat, cover for about 10 minutes, stirring several times. Add ½ tsp. of pepper, curry, dill, orange zest, juice and stock. Bring to a boil, then simmer, partially covered, until the rice is cooked about 25 minutes. Cool briefly, then puree most of the soup and return to the pot. Taste for salt, season with pepper, garnish with finely chopped parsley and serve.

Recipe by: Rachel Enright

VEGAN – GLUTEN FREE

Soups

Coconut Vegetable

Serves 4-6

Ingredients:
Coconut Milk Mixture:
¼ medium Red onion
1 ½ Tbsp. Ginger, grated
½ Tbsp. Garlic, minced
½ Red bell pepper, chopped
1 ½ tsp. oil
1 can Coconut milk
Blended Vegetable Mixture:
½ Onion, chopped
1 clove Garlic, minced
1 Carrot, diced
2 Potatoes, diced
1 Yam, diced
1 Celery stalk, diced
1 Artichoke, sliced
1 ½ cups Mushrooms, sliced
1 cup Cabbage, chopped
1 cup Corn, frozen
1 Leek, sliced
2 cans Coconut milk

Preparation:
Saute Coconut Milk Mixture ingredients (minus coconut milk) until very soft. Add coconut milk. Simmer for 15-40 minutes. (The longer you simmer, the more the flavors blend) Puree and set aside. In a separate large pot, saute Blended Vegetable Mixture. Cook for about 10 minutes, until onions are translucent and mushrooms ae soft. Add ¾ cup of water and coconut milk to cover the contents. Now add Coconut Milk Mixture to pot. Bring to a boil until potatoes are soft. Add 1 handful of Cilantro, basil leaves (chopped) lemon juice, salt and pepper to taste.

Recipe by: Rachel Enright

VEGAN – GLUTEN FREE – PROTEIN RICH

Corn Chowder

Serves 6-8

Ingredients:

3 ½ cups Yukon Gold potatoes, diced (peel if desired)
7 cups Vegetable broth
6 cups Sweet corn
1 large Onion, chopped
2 tsp. Corn or Vegetable oil
2 Bay leaves
1 tsp. Rosemary
1 tsp. Thyme
½ tsp. Salt
1 tsp. Pepper

Preparation:

In a large soup pot, heat oil. Add onions, rosemary and thyme. Saute till onions are translucent. Add potatoes, vegetable broth, corn and bay leaves. Bring to a boil and reduce heat.

Simmer for 20 minutes. Remove bay leaves. Blend between half and all the soup in a blender or mash with a potato masher until soup is thick. Stir in salt and pepper to taste and serve immediately.

Recipe by: Marti Waite

VEGAN – PROTEIN RICH

 Soups

Gumbo

Serves 6-8

Ingredients:
1 cup white Flour
¾ cup Vegetable oil
1 medium Onion, diced
1 large Bell pepper, diced
4 stalks Celery, diced
3 Tomatoes, diced
6 cups Hot water
1 Tbsp. Paprika
1 Tbsp. Salt
¼ tsp. Cayenne
6 Bay leaves
1 ½ Tbsp. Thyme
2 cups Mushrooms, sliced
1 package extra firm tofu, drained and cubed
Pinch of Oregano
Pinch of Chili Powder
Pinch of Cumin

Preparation:
Preheat oven to 400. Drizzle vegetable oil over the cubed tofu and sprinkle with oregano, chili powder, garlic powder and cumin. Toss gently and bake for 40-45 minutes, flipping tofu once, until it is crispy and brown.

Meanwhile, heat ¾ cups vegetable oil and add to flour. Stir constantly until it is a very dark brown, almost burning (a very dark roux is the secret to good gumbo). When roux is dark, immediately add the onion, bell pepper, celery and tomatoes and saute for 10 miutes, stirring constantly. Add mushrooms, cook for about 5 minutes. Then add water and spices. Bring to a boil, lower to medium heat and cook for 45 minutes.

Recipe by: Rachel Enright

VEGAN – GLUTEN FREE – PROTEIN RICH

Hungarian Mushroom

Serves 6-8

Ingredients:

½ cup Margarine
2 pounds Mushrooms, sliced
1 Tbsp. Dried dill
1 ½ Tbsp. Paprika
2 Tbsp. Tamari
1 quart Vegetable broth
2 cups Rice milk
1/3 cup Cornstarch
Salt and Pepper to taste
1 Tbsp. Lemon juice
1/3 bunch Parsley
(Sour cream – if desired on the side)

Preparation:

Melt the margarine is a large pot over medium heat. Saute the mushrooms for around five minutes. Stir in the dill, paprika, tamari and vegetable broth. Reduce heat to low, cover and simmer for 15 minutes. In a separate bowl whisk the rice milk and cornstarch together. Pour this into the soup and stir well to blend. Cover and simmer for 15 more minutes, stirring occasionally. Finally, stir in the salt, ground black pepper, lemon juice and parsley. Mix together and allow toheat through over low heat, about 3-5 minutes. Do not allow to boil.
Serve with sour cream on the side if desired.

Recipe by: Rachel Enright

VEGAN – GLUTEN FREE – PROTEIN RICH

Lentil Veggie

Serves 6-8

Ingredients:

Olive Oil – for saute
1 ½ Onions, finely diced
½ Garlic clove, minced
Salt and Pepper to taste
2 Tbsp. + 2 tsp. Tomato paste
¼ cup Celery diced
¼ cup Carrot, diced
1 Bay leaf
Scant ½ cup Parsley
1 cup + 6 Tbsp. Green lentils
1 quart Vegetable broth
1 ¼ Tbsp. Dijon mustard
1 ¼ Tbsp. Red wine vinegar

Preparation:

Cook lentils separately till they are almost done.   Heat oil in a soup pot over high heat. Add onions and saute until clear.   Work the tomato paste into the onion and then add garlic celery, carrots, bay leaves, parsley and cook for around 3 minutes.
Add cooked lentils, water and broth.   Bring to a boil. Lower the heat and simmer, partially covered until the lentils are **completely tender.** Stir in mustard and vinegar. Check the seasoning and remove bay leaf before serving.

Recipe by: Ben Waite

VEGAN – PROTEIN RICH

 Soups

Minestrone

Serves 6-8

Ingredients:

Olive Oil – for saute
1 ½ Onions, chopped
5 ¾ cups Vegetable broth
3 cups Zucchini, diced
3 cups Carrots, diced
2 ¼ cup White beans, cooked
1 ½ cups Celery diced
2 ¼ tsp. Basil, dried
½ tsp. Oregano, dried
½ tsp. Salt
¼ tsp. Black Pepper
28 oz. can Diced Tomatoes
1 ½ cups Elbow pasta, uncooked

Preparation:

Heat oil in large cooking pot over medium-high heat. Add chopped onion and saute until just lightly browned. Add broth, zucchini, carrots, beans, celery, basil, oregano, salt, pepper, diced tomatoes and garlic. Bring to a boil. Reduce heat, cover and simmer for around 25 minutes, stirring occasionally.
In a separate pot, cook pasta until done. Drain and add to soup.

Recipe by: Marti Waite

VEGAN – GLUTEN FREE

Pea Soup with Tarragon

Serves 6-8

Ingredients:

Olive Oil – for saute
4 ea. Leeks, white and light green parts thinly sliced
2 cloves Garlic, thinly minced
1 quart Vegetable broth
2 cups Water
¾ quart Frozen peas, thawed
1 Tbsp. Tarragon leaves
Salt and Pepper to taste

Preparation:

Wash leeks thoroughly. Heat oil in soup pot over medium heat. Add leaks and saute until soft. Stir in garlic and cook one minute more. Add vegetable broth and water and bring to a simmer. Cook 15 minutes and then stir in peas and cook another minute. Remove from heat and let cool for about 30 minutes. Puree soup in food processor with tarragon leaves until smooth. Season with salt and pepper. Pour back into pot and simmer until warmed.

Recipe by: Marti Waite

GLUTEN FREE

Potato Leek and Arugula

Serves 6-8

Ingredients:

2 Tbsp. Butter or margarine
1 ½ Tbsp. Oil
1 Onion, chopped
2 ½ ea. Leek, chopped
1 ½ cloves Garlic, chopped
2 ea. Potatoes, diced
6 cups Water
¼ box Arugula
½ cup Heavy cream or coconut milk
Salt and Pepper to taste

Preparation:

Wash the leeks thoroughly. In a large soup pot, heat oil. Add onions, butter, garlic, leeks and saute until onions are translucent. Add potatoes and water. Bring to a boil and reduce heat. Simmer until all vegetables are tender. Turn off the heat, and add fresh arugula into the soup. Blend HALF of the soup in a blender. Mix with non-blended soup. Stir in cream (or coconut milk) and salt and pepper to taste.

Recipe by: Marti Waite

VEGAN – GLUTEN FREE

Roasted Zucchini

Serves 6-8

Ingredients:

Vegetable oil – for roasting
1 12 ea. Yellow onions, sliced
3 pounds Zucchini, trimmed and sliced
1 ½ quarts Vegetable broth
1 ½ cups Soy milk
½ Tbsp. Curry powder
Salt and Pepper to taste

Preparation:

Preheat oven to 400. Slice onion and zucchini. Toss with oil and spread flat onto a cookie sheet. Season with salt and pepper. Roast until brown. Puree the roasted vegetables in a food processor or blender. Place into a soup pot. Add veggie stock to soup pot and bring to a boil. Add cream and curry powder and simmer for a few minutes. Serve with tortilla chips. If non-vegan, can add grated Parmesan.

Recipe by: Rachel Enright

VEGAN – PROTEIN RICH

Spinach Artichoke

Serves 6-8

Ingredients:

FOR CREAM
4 cans White beans
2 cups Unsweetened Almond milk
8 Tbsp. Lemon, juiced
5 ½ Tbsp. Nutritional Yeast
3 ½ White Miso
1 tsp. Mustard powder
FOR SOUP
4 ea. Shallots, chopped
3 Medium sized garlic cloves, minced
4 cans Artichoke hearts
4 cans Spinach leaves
3 ½ tsp. Dried Basil
2 tsp. Dried Oregano
7 cups Vegetable broth
2 cups Water
Salt and Pepper – to taste
2 tsp. Olive Oil

Preparation:

FOR CREAM: Rinse and drain cans of great northern white beans and artichoke hearts. In a food processor, combine ingredients for the cream and blend until smooth. Set aside.

FOR SOUP: In a large pot heat the olive oil over medium heat for 2 minutes. Add shallots and garlic and saute until fragrant and the garlic is translucent. Add the artichokes, basil and oregano and saute for 3-4 minutes. Add the spinach, vegetable stock and water. Mix well. Put lid on and bring to boil, stirring until spinach cooks down. Once boiling, crack lid and bring to simmer for about 12 minutes. Then remove from heat. Use immersion blender and pulse till chunky. Pour in the cream mixture until combined. Salt and pepper to taste, Return to simmer about 12 minutes.

Recipe by: Ruth Nucera

VEGAN –GLUTEN FREE – PROTEIN RICH

 Soups

Tuscan Bean

Serves 6-8

Ingredients:

1 cup Cannellini beans, soaked overnight
1 Tbsp. olive oil
½ cup Yellow onion, diced
3 cloves Garlic, minced
1 cup canned Tomatoes, diced
2 cups Water
3 sprigs fresh Thyme
1 Bay leaf
Pinch of red Chili flakes
Salt and Pepper to taste

Preparation:

Place the beans in a medium pot, add water to cover by 2 inches and bring to a boil. Turn the heat down. Let simmer for 45-60 minutes or until tender.

In a large soup pot, heat the olive oil over medium heat. Add the onion and garlic. Season with salt and freshly ground black pepper to taste. Add the diced tomatoes, the cooked and drained beans and water. Season with thyme, bay leaf, red chili flakes, salt and pepper. Cook for 20 minutes.

Serve soup in large bowls with optional grated cheese and slice of toast.

Recipe by: Rachel Enright

Salads & Dressings

From romaine to spring mix to everything in between, the base for having a great salad is great lettuce. In our mission to be a center with a good heart, we try always to buy local and organic lettuce to use as the base of our delicious salads.

But a salad is not a salad without a great dressing. Some of our most requested recipes throughout the years have been our salad dressing recipes.

Salads are served both for lunch and dinner at Land of Medicine Buddha so it is important to make sure they are as satisfying as possible

This section includes both dressings and complete salads for your enjoyment.

Salads & Dressings

Classic Caesar Salad and Dressing

Serves 4

Ingredients:
3 cloves garlic, peeled
3/4 cup mayonnaise
4 Tbsp. capers
3 oz. caper juice
1/4 cup + 2 Tbsp. grated Parmesan cheese, divided
1 tsp vegetarian Worcestershire sauce
1 tsp Dijon mustard
1 Tbsp. lemon juice
Salt to taste - ground black pepper to taste
1 1/2 cup olive oil
2 cups day-old bread, cubed
1 head romaine lettuce, torn into bite-size pieces

Preparation:
Combine garlic in a food processor or blender with mayonnaise, capers, caper juice, 4 tablespoons of the Parmesan cheese, Worcestershire sauce, mustard, and lemon juice and blend while slowly adding 1 cup of olive oil. Season to taste with salt and black pepper. Refrigerate until ready to use.

Heat oven to 350. Toss the cubed bread with remaining olive oil and coat evenly. Continue tossing and add salt and a generous portion of fresh cracked black peppercorn. Pour onto a sheet pan and spread evenly and place in oven for approximately 8-9 minutes or until golden brown. Remove from oven and set aside.

Place lettuce in a large bowl. Toss with dressing, remaining Parmesan cheese, and seasoned bread cubes. Serve immediately.

Recipe by: Rachel Enright

VEGAN – GLUTEN FREE

Salads & Dressings

Cilantro-Lime Vinaigrette

Makes 2.5 cups

Ingredients:

½ cup Red onion, quartered
1/3 cup Lime juice
1/3 cup Lemon juice
1 clove Garlic
2 Tbsp. + 2 tsp. Agave nectar
2 Tbsp. + 2 tsp. Brown rice vinegar
1 Tbsp. Coriander
1 tsp. Salt
½ Tbsp. Cumin
Pinch of Cayenne
1 cup Olive oil
1 cup Cilantro

Preparation:

Combine all ingredients in a food processor and blend until thoroughly mixed.

Recipe by: Marti Waite

GLUTEN FREE

Salads & Dressings

Feta Ranch

Makes 2 cups

Ingredients:
¾ cup Sour cream
¾ cup Mayonnaise
¼ cup Lemon juice
¼ cup Feta cheese
1 tsp. dried dill
6 Tbsp. Oregano
½ tsp. Onion powder
½ clove Garlic, minced
¼ tsp. Granulated garlic
1 Green onion, finely chopped
Salt and Pepper to taste

Preparation:
Mix ingredients in a bowl until completely blended
and refrigerate for at least an hour. Serve.

Recipe by: Rachel Enright

VEGAN

Salads & Dressings

French Grated Carrot Salad

Serves 4-6

Ingredients:

1 ½ pounds Carrots, peeled
1 Tbsp. Dijon mustard
1 ½ Tbsp. Lemon juice
¼ cup Olive oil
1 Tbsp. Honey
Salt and Pepper – to taste
2 Tbsp. + 2 tsp. Parsley, chopped
1 ½ Tbsp. Shallots, finely chopped

Preparation:

Grate carrots in food processor and set aside. Combine
Dijon, lemon juice, oil, honey and salt and pepper in a
salad bowl.   Add carrots, parsley and shallots.   Toss to
combine. Cover and refrigerate until serving.
Note: Replace honey with agave to make vegan dressing.

Recipe by: Marti Waite

VEGAN – GLUTEN FREE

Salads & Dressings

Green Goddess Dressing

Serves 6

Ingredients:
1 cup packed Parsley
1 cup packed Spinach
1/2 a Zucchini
1 clove Garlic
1/4 cup Apple cider vinegar
1/2 cup Olive oil
1/2 a Lemon
Salt & Pepper

Preparation:
In a blender combine parsley, spinach, zucchini, garlic, vinegar and blend till smooth and even.   Add oil and taste to see if you need more tartness. If so, add lemon juice.   Salt and pepper to taste and serve.

Recipe by: Brian Espanoza

GLUTEN FREE – PRECEPT
FRIENDLY

Salads & Dressings

Honey Mustard Vinaigrette

Makes 2 cups

Ingredients:
1/3 cup Apple cider vinegar
1/3 cup Dijon mustard
1/3 cup Honey
1 cup Vegetable oil
Salt – to taste

Preparation:
Combine all ingredients in a food processor or blender and mix until well blended. Serve.

Recipe by Mari Waite

GLUTEN FREE

Salads & Dressings

Mayan Dressing

Makes 2 cups

Ingredients:
1 cup Orange juice
2 Tbsp. Orange zest
2 cloves Garlic
1 pinch Allspice
¼ cup Honey
1/8 cup Fresh cilantro or basil
Salt – to taste
1/8 cup Olive oil
½ ea. Lime
¼ ea. Lemon
Pinch of Cayenne

Preparation:
Combine all ingredients in a food processor or blender and mix until well blended. Note: Replace honey with agave to make vegan dressing.   Serve.

Recipe by: Eric Oztochane

VEGAN – GLUTEN FREE

Salads & Dressings

Parsley Salad

Serves 6-8

Ingredients:

3 ½ bunches Parsley, chopped
1 pound Almonds or sun flower seeds, chopped
½ pound Raisins, chopped
2 ea. Lemons, juiced
2 peels of Lemon zest
A "glug" of Olive oil
2 Tbsp. Brown sugar
Salt and Pepper – to taste

Preparation:

Mix lemon juice, lemon zest, olive oil and brown sugar in a large bowl. Add parsley, almonds and raisins. Toss well. Let salad sit for at least 30 minutes for the flavors to meld.

Recipe by: Marti Waite

VEGAN – GLUTEN FREE

Salads & Dressings

Quinoa Salad

Serves 4

Ingredients:

1 ½ cups of Water
¾ cup uncooked Quinoa
2 Carrots, peeled in small cubes
¾ large Green bell pepper, diced
¾ large Red bell pepper, diced
2 stalks of Celery, diced
¼ cup plus 2 Tbsp. Kalamata olives, chopped
3 Tbsp. fresh Parsley, chopped
3 Tbsp. fresh Chives, chopped
¼ tsp. salt
½ cup fresh Lemon juice
2 ¼ cup Red wine vinegar
3 Tbsp. Olive oil

Preparation:

Bring the water and salt to a boil in a saucepan.   Stir in the quinoa, reduce heat to medium-low, cover and simmer until the quinoa is tender and the water has been absorbed; about 15-20 minutes.   Scrape the quinoa into a large bowl.

Gently stir the carrots, bell peppers, olives, celery, parsley, chives, parsley and salt into the quinoa.   Drizzle with the lemon juice, red wine vinegar and olive oil.   Stir until evenly mixed.   Serve warm or refrigerate and serve cold.

Recipe by: Brian Espanoza

GLUTEN FREE

Salads & Dressings

Thai Peanut Dressing

Makes 2 cups

Ingredients:

¾ cup Peanut Butter
6 Tbsp. Tamari
¼ small can Coconut milk
½ tsp. Sesame oil
1 ½ Tbsp. Fresh ginger
1 ½ cloves Garlic, peeled
2 Tbsp. Red wine vinegar
½ ea. Lime juice
½ ea. Lime zest
2 tsp. Brown sugar
½ Tbsp. Honey
½ Tbsp. Hot sauce (example Sriracha)
½ cup Water

Preparation:

Chop the ginger. Peel the garlic. Blend all ingredients in a blender until well mixed. Serve

Recipe by Rachel Enright

Main Dishes

One of the joys at Land of Medicine Buddha is seeing the happy faces of the guests lining up in front of the serving tables at lunch time.

Since lunch is our biggest meal here, we strive to pack it full of the most awesome and healthy tastes, which we are happy to share with you in the following recipes.

These recipes go from simple vegetarian dishes such as white beans and greens to our most requested recipe; enchiladas

And we cover the globe from American to Mexican, to French, Italian, Spanish, Asian and of course Indian cuisine.

GLUTEN FREE – PROTEIN RICH

Main Dishes

Black Bean and Zucchini Chilaquiles

Serves 6-8

Ingredients:

Olive Oil – for saute
1 ¼ Onions, chopped
1 ¼ Green bell pepper, diced
3 5 oz. Tomatoes, diced
2 ½ tsp. Chili powder
1 ¼ tsp. Dried oregano
2/3 tsp. Cumin
3 1/8 cups Black beans, cooked
1 ½ ea. Zucchini
5 oz. Mild green chilis
12 Corn flour tortillas
1 1/8 pound Cheddar cheese

Preparation:

Quarter and slice the zucchini. Preheat oven to 400. Lightly oil baking dish. Heat the oil in a large saucepan. Saute the onions until translucent.   Add the bell peppers and continue until they are softened.   Stir in tomatoes, seasonings, beans, zucchinis and chili peppers. Bring to a simmer then simmer for around 5 minutes.   Layer in the baking pan: half of the tortillas, half the tomato black bean mixture and half the cheese. Repeat. Bake for 15-20 minutes or until cheese is bubbly.   Let stand for 10-15 minutes, then cut into squares.   Good to serve with sour cream or yogurt on the side.

Recipe by Vimal Dass

GLUTEN FREE – PROTEIN RICH

Main Dishes

Coconut Vegetable Curry

Serves 6-8

Ingredients:

FOR SAUCE
Oil
1 ea. Onion, diced
1 ½ cloves Garlic, minced
1 small Tomatoes, from a can
1 small Coconut milk
Cayenne pepper
½ tsp. Tumeric
¼ tsp. Garam masala
½ tsp. Cumin
½ tsp. Coriander
1 tsp. Mustard seeds
FOR VEGGIES
1 package Tofu, sliced, pressed and grilled
1 cup Chickpeas, cooked
1 bunch Broccoli, cut into florets and stems
1 ½ medium ea. Butternut squash, cubed

Preparation:

FOR SAUCE: Heat oil in pan. Add onion, garlic, saute until golden.   Add all the spices, tomatoes and coconut milk. Reduce heat and simmer 15 minutes. FOR VEGGIES: Cube and grill tofu.   Briefly cook broccoli in water.   Bake squash in oven at 400 until soft. Mix it all with sauce and cooked chickpeas. Season with salt and pepper.

Recipe by: Vimal Dass

31

VEGAN – GLUTEN FREE – PROTEIN RICH

Main Dishes

Dahl and Rice
A la Medicine Buddha

Serves 6-8

Ingredients:

2 ½ cups Red lentils
7 ½ cups Water or vegetable stock
1 Tbsp. Ground cumin
½ Tbsp. Ground tumeric
1 Tbsp. Fresh ginger, grated
¾ Tbsp. Green curry paste
Bragg's Nutritional yeast – to taste
2 ½ cups Bastami Rice
Optional: dollop of sour cream or yogurt

Preparation:

Place lentils and water in pot. Cover and bring to a boil. Regularly skim foam from top of boiling water. Reduce heat to low and simmer about 30 minutes. Add cumin, turmeric and ginger to lentils while they are cooking. As the dahl cooks, make the basmati rice.   When lentils are cooked, add curry paste and Bragg's. Simmer together for 10 minutes. Serve over rice.

Optional: A dollop of Sour Cream or Yogurt is nice on top after plating.

Recipe by: Vimal Dass

VEGAN – GLUTEN FREE – PROTEIN RICH

Main Dishes

Enchiladas

Serves 6-8

Ingredients:

FOR SAUCE
¼ cup Corn starch
1/3 cup Water (cold)
1/8 cup Vegetable Oil
1 ea. Medium onion, diced
1 ¾ Tbsp. Ground cumin
1 ¾ Tbsp. Chili powder
15 oz. Tomato sauce
Salt – to taste
2 cups Water
FOR ENCHILADAS
Vegetable oil – for saute
2 pounds Firm tofu, drained and crumbled
16 Corn tortillas
1ea. Medium onion, diced finely
1 ea. Red bell peppers, diced finely
1 cup Cilantro, coarsely chopped
2 Tbsp. Cumin
2 Tbsp. Chili powder
1 ½ Tbsp. Tamari

Preparation:

Make enchilada sauce first. Dissolve cornstarch in water. Heat oil in saucepan until shimmering. Add onions. Saute until onions are translucent. Add cumin, chili powder and cornstarch mix, whisking until brown and thickened. Slowly stir in tomato sauce and water, mixing well. Reduce heat to low and simmer for about 15 minutes. **(continued on next page...)**

33

Main Dishes

(Continued from previous page) Season with salt to taste. Remove from heat, but keep warm.

FOR ENCHILADAS: Preheat oven to 375. On griddle, heat oil until shimmering. Add tofu and cook until brown and somewhat crispy and its liquid has evaporated. Once brown, add 2/3 of the onions and ½ of the red bell peppers. Stir and add cilantro, cumin and chili powder, mix well. Add tamari and mix well. Saute until the onions and red bell peppers begin to soften. Add a couple of tablespoons of water if it seems parched, but oil should be dry. It should resemble crisp, browned bits of meat. While the tofu mixture is cooking, wrap the tortillas tightly in aluminum foil and place in the oven for about 10 minutes. In a shallow pan, add 1/3 of the sauce to coat the bottom of pan. Unwrap the hot tortillas and place in the sauce to coat them. Flip over to coat both sides. Add filling and roll tightly, keeping seam side down. Repeat until tortillas are done. Pour the remaining sauce on top of the tortillas and sprinkle with the remaining uncooked bell pepper and onion. Bake until the sauce is bubbling.

Can be served with sour cream and cheese on the side.

Recipe by: Vimal Dass

PROTEIN RICH

Main Dishes

Magnificent Mushroom Burgers

Serves 6-8

Ingredients:

1 ¼ cup Portabella mushrooms
1 ¼ cup Cooked black beans
1 ¼ cup Broccoli, minced
¾ cup Red onions, minced
2 Eggs, beaten
¼ cup Vegetable Oil
1 ¼ cups Bread crumbs
Pinch of Salt
Pinch of Pepper
¾ Tbsp. Worcestershire sauce
¼ cup Garlic, minced
¾ cup Parmesan cheese

Preparation:

Remove gills and cube the mushrooms. Rinse and divide the beans. Preheat oven to 400. Line baking sheet with well oiled parchment paper. In mixing bowl add ½ of the beans and mash them. Add in the mushrooms, rest of the beans, broccoli, garlic, onion, Worcestershire sauce, salt and pepper. Mix until just coated. Add the eggs, oil, cheese and bread crumbs and mix gently until combined. Scoop ½ cup portions and gently shape into a burger while pressing together until mixture holds. Place on cookie sheet with space between the individual burgers. Bake for 10 minutes. Flip patties, bake for an additional 10 minutes. Serve on bun with the usual burger fixings.

Recipe by: Vimal Dass

PROTEIN RICH

Main Dishes

Mushroom Cutlets with Red Pepper Sauce

Serves 8

Ingredients:

FOR CUTLETS:
Same burger ingredients on previous page
FOR SAUCE:
4 cups Cashews
8 Red peppers, roasted
4 cups Vegetable broth
¼ cup Rice wine vinegar
4 cloves Garlic
Salt and Pepper

Preparation:

FOR CUTLETS: Same preparation as burgers on previous page.   Scoop ½ cup portions and gently shape into cutlet shape; pressing together until mixture holds.   Place on cookie sheet with space between individual cutlets. Bake for about 10 minutes.   Flip cutlets and bake for about additional 10 minutes. FOR RED PEPPER SAUCE: Roast the peppers on a burner or in oven for 15 minutes at 400.   Place in a sealed container for 15 minutes.   Peel in a bowl of water.   Some charred flakes are okay. Combine all ingredients in a mixer.   Nut sauces thicken quickly. This is not a reductions sauce, so it needs to be warmed not boiled.   Serve warm over top of cutlets.

Recipe by: Vimal Dass

VEGAN – GLUTEN FREE – PROTEIN RICH   Main Dishes

Orange Glazed Tempeh

Serves 6-8

Ingredients:

2 cups Orange juice
1/8 cup Ginger, grated
1 1/3 Tbsp. Tamari
1 1/3 Tbsp. Maple Syrup
1 tsp. Coriander, ground
1 ¼ pound Tempeh
1/8 cup Olive oil
1 Lime
Cilantro (optional)

Preparation:

Put orange juice in mixing bowl. Squeeze grated ginger over the bowl to extract the juices, then throw away the pulp.   Add Tamari, maple syrup and ground coriander. Mix and set aside. Cut the tempeh into thin, bite sized pieces.   Put olive oil in a large frying pan over medium-high heat.   When the oil is hot, but not smoking, add the tempeh, fry for 5 minutes or until golden underneath.   Turn and cook the other side for 5 minutes or until golden.   Pour the orange juice mixture into the pan and simmer for about 10 minutes or until the sauce has reduced into a thick glaze. Turn the tempeh once more during this time and spoon the sauce over the tempeh from time to time. Before serving, squeeze the lime and drizzle the remaining sauce over the dish, and add cilantro (if desired).

Recipe by: Vimal Dass

VEGAN – GLUTEN FREE

Main Dishes

Pad Thai

Serves 6-8

Ingredients:

1 box Rice noodles
½ cup Tamari
6 Tbsp. Lime juice
½ cup Peanut butter
1 tsp. Hot sauce
6 Tbsp. Sugar
1 1/8 pound Tofu, cubed
1 ea. Onion, diced
¼ cup Sesame oil
¼ cup Bean sprouts
½ cup Peanuts, chopped
Green onions, sliced - garnish

Preparation:

FOR NOODLES: Boil water, add noodles and cook for 5 minutes. Transfer to cold water. FOR SAUCE: Whisk together the Tamari, peanut butter, lime juice, hot sauce and sugar. In a wok or skillet, saute the tofu and onions in sesame oil for minute or two, stirring frequently. Add the cooked noodles, peanut butter and soy sauce mixture. Stir well, and allow sauce to thicken as it cooks for about 3 minutes. Transfer to a serving plate. Garnish with green onions. FOR SIDES: Serve with peanuts and bean sprouts on the side.

Recipe by: Vimal Dass

PROTEIN RICH

Main Dishes

Pasta with No-Meat Balls

Serves 6-8

Ingredients:

2 ½ Tbsp. Olive oil
1 ea. Onion, diced finely
2 cups Mushrooms, sliced
3 cloves Garlic, chopped
1 ½ packages Firm tofu, drained well and crumbled
1 ½ Eggs
2 cups Bread crumbs
Flour – to coat the "meat" balls
1 box Pasta
Red pepper flakes
Ground black pepper, salt
Parsley, finely chopped
Oregano
Lemon zest

Preparation:

Preheat oven to 450. In a pot, saute onion, garlic and salt.
When soft, add mushrooms and red pepper flakes. Raise the
heat to high and cook, stirring frequently until mushrooms have
given off their juices and are lightly caramelized. Transfer
mushroom mixture to food processor or blender. Add tofu, egg
and more salt. Pulse to combine. Add bread crumbs and
parsley and pulse to combine again. Scrape mixture into bread
bowl and season with black pepper. Coat plate with flour. With
wet hands, for 1 ½ inch balls with the tofu mixture. Lightly coat
the balls in the flour and place them onto an **oiled** baking sheet.
Place balls in the oven and cook until all are browned on one
side; about 20 minutes. Remove from oven, turn balls and place
in oven again to brown the other side. Add Marinara Sauce (**see
next page**) into pan. Place balls in pan. Pour rest of sauce over
top and add parmesan cheese and roast till bubbly. Serve with
pasta.

Recipe by: Marti Waite

VEGAN – GLUTEN FREE

Main Dishes

Homemade Marinara Sauce
(See previous page for No-Meat Balls)

Serves 6-8

Ingredients:
1/8 cup Oil
1 ea. Onion, sliced
2 cloves Garlic, sliced
1 ea. Carrots, peeled
½ ea. Celery, sliced
½ can Canned tomatoes
Salt and Pepper – to taste

Preparation:
Chop the carrots into small pieces. Heat the oil in a pot over medium-high heat. Saute the onions, garlic, carrots and celery, stirring about 8 minutes. Add the tomatoes with salt and pepper and bring to a boil.   Reduce heat and simmer uncovered for about 20 minutes, or until slightly thickened. Blend all in the blender. Pour half into pan. Add No-Meat Balls (**see recipe on previous page**). Pour rest over top.   Add cheese if desired and cook until bubbly or caramelized.   Serve over side of pasta.

Recipe by: Marti Waite

GLUTEN FREE

Penne with Gorgonzola and Walnuts

Serves 6-8

Ingredients:
½ pound Gorgonzola
1 1/8 oz. Margarine
6 Tbsp. Walnuts
¾ tsp. Lemon juice
Olive oil – for saute
Pinch of Black pepper
½ clove Garlic
6 Tbsp. Half and Half
1 1/3 pound Penne

Preparation:
Finely chop walnuts and roast. Set aside. Mince garlic, fry for 30 seconds in olive oil over low heat. Set aside. Cut gorgonzola into pieces. Put on water, bring to a rolling boil, add 1 Tablespoon of salt and pasta. Stir. While pasta is cooking, put garlic in butter and cook over low heat. As it melts, add the cheese. Add Half and Half and keep stirring. When it becomes a sauce, add lemon juice and the walnuts. Drain pasta, saving ½ cup of pasta water. Pour sauce over pasta. Add parsley and pepper. Mix well. Add reserved pasta water if sauce is too thick.

Recipe by: Marti Waite

GLUTEN FREE – PROTEIN RICH – PRECEPT FRIENDLY

Main Dishes

Portabella Tacos

Serves 6-8

Ingredients:
1/3 cup Vegetable oil
2 Tbsp and 2 tsp. Balsamic vinegar
1 tsp. Black pepper
8 ea. Portabella caps
16 Corn tortillas
Cabbage, shredded – for side
Sour cream – for side
Cheese – for side

Preparation:
Preheat griddle.   Cut stems off mushrooms.   Combine oil, balsamic vinegar and pepper.   Marinate portabellas in oil and vinegar for ½ hour.   Shred cabbage, grate cheese. Grill mushrooms on the griddle about 3-5 minutes per side. Slice mushrooms into strips.   Lightly warm corn tortillas on griddle. Serve mushrooms and tortillas on separate plates along with cabbage, cheese, sour cream. Note – Can also be served with Salsa Fresca (see recipe on page 71)

Recipe by: Vimal Dass

GLUTEN FREE – PROTEIN RICH

Main Dishes

Quinoa Frittata with Herbs and Feta

Serves 6-8

Ingredients:

8 Eggs
1 cup cooked Quinoa
¼ tsp. Nutmeg
½ cup Green onions or shallots, chopped
2 Tbsp. Fresh herbs
¼ cup Parsley
¼ cup Feta, crumbled
1/8 cup Parmesan
Salt and Pepper – to taste

Preparation:

Preheat oven to 375. Beat the eggs together with the quinoa. Add the nutmeg, salt and pepper to taste. On the stove, over medium heat, saute onions to soften for about a minute. Add onions to egg mixture along with the herbs. Pour into greased cooking pan. Sprinkle with cheese. Bake until golden brown and center is set.

Recipe by: Marti Waite

GLUTEN FREE

Main Dishes

Ratatouille

Serves 6

Ingredients:

3 Zucchinis, cut into 1" diagonal pieces
2 Red bell peppers, cut into 1" squares
1 lg. Eggplant, unpeeled and cut into 1" cubes
2 Carrots, cut into 1" diagonal pieces
1 Yellow onion, cut into 1" cubes
1/4 cup Parsley, diced
1/4 cup Basil, diced
1/2 cup Tomato paste
1/4 cup Honey
Salt and Pepper
4 Tbsp. Vegetable oil

Preparation:

Preheat oven to 350. Cut all vegetables and toss together with the oil and lightly salt and pepper. Spread onto a sheet pan and place into oven for 20-25 minutes, until vegetables are caramelized and cooked through, but still holding their shape.

Once vegetables have caramelized, take them out of the oven and toss in the tomato paste, honey, and fresh diced herbs.   Salt and pepper to taste. Serve in casserole, over pasta, or in grilled sandwiches.

Recipe by: Brian Espanoza

VEGAN – GLUTEN FREE

Main Dishes

Shepherd's Pie

Serves 6-8

Ingredients:

3 pounds Potatoes, peeled and chopped
1/8 cup Coconut oil
6 Tbsp. Non-dairy milk
½ tsp. Garlic Powder
1/8 cup Olive oil
1 ea. Onion, finely chopped
3 ea. Garlic, minced
4 ea. Carrots
2 ea. Parsnips (or other root vegetable)
4 ea. Celery stalks
1 ¼ cup Vegetable broth
2 tsp. Thyme
½ tsp. Oregano
3 Tbsp. Flour (white or Gluten Free)
Salt & Pepper - to taste

Preparation:

Preheat oven to 425 and lightly oil baking pan. Place peeled and chopped potatoes into large pot and add water, 2 inches above potatoes.   Bring to a boil and then simmer on low for about 30 minutes until very tender. Meanwhile, prepare the vegetable filling.   Chop carrots, parsnips and celery. Chop the onions, mince the garlic and add to a skillet along with the oil. Cook on low for about 5-7 minutes Add in chopped vegetables. Cook on medium-low for about 15 minutes.   When potatoes are done cooking, drain and add back to the pot.   Add the coconut oil, milk and seasonings and mash well. Set aside.   In a small bowl, whisk together the broth, spices and flour.   Add this liquid mixture to the vegetables in the skillet and stir well.   Add salt and pepper to taste.   Cook for about 8 minutes until thickened.   Add more broth if needed.   Season to taste. Scoop vegetable mixture into serving pan. Spread on the mashed potato mixture and garnish with paprika, etc. Bake at 425 for about 35 minutes. Or until golden bubbly.   Allow 20 minutes to cook before serving.

Recipe by: Rachel Enright

VEGAN

Main Dishes

Spring Thyme Spaghetti

Serves 6-8

Ingredients:
1/8 cup Olive oil
1 large bunch Scallions, thinly sliced with the greens
1 Tbsp. Lemon zest
1 Tbsp. Fresh Thyme, finely chopped
Salt and Pepper to taste
2 pounds asparagus
¼ cup chopped walnuts or toasted sun seeds
2 Tbsp. and 2 tsp. Parsley, chopped
1/4 cup Snipped Chives
Parmesan cheese - optional
2 pounds Spaghetti

Preparation:
Heat water for pasta. While waiting, heat half the oil in a wide skillet over low heat.   Add the scallions, lemon zest, thyme and a few pinches of salt.   Cook slowly, stirring occasionally. Meanwhile, remove tough ends of asparagus and slice 3 inch tips off.   Then slice the remaining stalks diagonally or make a roll cut.   When water boils, salt it, add asparagus and cook until partially tender, 3-4 minutes.   Scoot it out, add it to the scallions and continue cooking on low heat.

Cook the pasta, add it to the pan with some of the water clinging to the strands. Raise the heat and stir in the remaining oil, nuts and seeds, parsley, chives and pepper to taste. Serve with parmesan on the side, if desired.

Recipe by: Marti Waite

GLUTEN FREE – PROTEIN RICH

Main Dishes

Tempeh Stir-Fry with Broccoli and Peppers

Serves 6-8

Ingredients:

1 pound Tempeh, cut into ½ inch pieces
¼ cup Tamari
2 Tbsp. and 2 tsp. Brown rice vinegar
3 cloves Garlic, minced
1 Tbsp. Ginger, peeled and minced
1 ½ pounds Broccoli, cut into florets
3 Tbsp. Water
2 tsp. Honey
2 tsp. Cornstarch
2 tsp. Olive oil
2 ea. Red peppers, sliced into strips

Preparation:

Stir Tamari, vinegar, garlic and ginger until blended. Add tempeh and marinate for 1 hour at room temperature. Steam broccoli until crisp-tender. Strain marinade from tempeh into mixing bowl. Add water, honey and cornstarch and mix. Saute tempeh and marinade. Add broccoli and marinade mix. Saute until broccoli is heated and sauce thickens. Transfer to serving pan. Serve and enjoy.

Recipe by: Vimal Dass

GLUTEN FREE – PRECEPT FRIENDLY

Three Baked Cheese Polenta

Serves 6-8

Ingredients:

6 cups Water
2 cups Polenta
1 ½ cup Mozzarella
1 cup Feta or blue cheese
½ cup Parmesan or Fontina cheese
1/8 cup Butter
Marinara Tomato Sauce****See page 40 for recipe

Preparation:

Preheat oven to 350. Prepare all ingredients before cooking polenta. When the polenta is cooked and very hot, begin the layering process. In sauce pan, bring water to a boil. Pour polenta slowly, while whisking constantly. Continue to whisk until mixture comes to a soft boil. Reduce heat to low and simmer, stirring often, until polenta is thick and cooked through**. When polenta is cooked, ladle 1/3 of cooked polenta into bottom of greased baking pan. With rubber spatula, spread to uniform thickness. Sprinkle ½ the butter and Parmesan over the polenta and butter. Ladle ½ of the remaining polenta over the cheese. Spread or sprinkle the remaining butter and Feta cheese. Ladle and spread the remaining polenta over the Feta layer. Spread with 1/2 the tomato sauce. Cover with foil and bake at 350 for 30 minutes. Remove foil, spread the remaining tomato sauce over the polenta. Sprinkle remaining Parmesan over sauce. Bake uncovered for 30 minutes. Let rest 15-30 minutes before serving. If polenta starts to seize up, slowly add more hot water and whisk to a boil until it liquefies again.

Recipe by: Marti Waite

VEGAN – GLUTEN FREE

Tofu with Aztec Mole

Serves 6

Ingredients:
4 lbs. extra firm Tofu
3 Tbsp. Chili powder (mild)
¼ cup Tamari
6 Tbsp. Vegetable Oil
¼ cup Onions, finely chopped
2 Tbsp. Unsweetened cocoa powder
1 ½ tsp. ground Cumin
4 Tbsp. Sesame seeds
¼ cup Peanuts
½ tsp. dried Garlic, minced
1 cup Tomato paste
¼ cup Agave nectar
1 Ancho chili
1 ½ cups Water

Preparation:
Preheat oven to 375. Prepare tofu for roasting by cutting tofu into 1 inch chunks. Place tofu in a large mixing bowl. Add Tamari, chili powder and 5 Tbsp. Oil. Sprinkle with salt and pepper, and toss it all together, mixing well. Spread across a large oiled sheet pan. Place pan into preheated oven for about 30 minutes until tofu is crisp and brown.

Meanwhile, prepare this traditional Aztec mole. Begin by heating a large sauce pan on the stove and add 1 Tbsp. oil. Once the oil is hot, add the onions. Cook until translucent. Then add garlic, sesame seeds, peanuts and cumin. Next add 1 ½ cups of water, the tomato paste and Ancho chili.
(continued on next page).

Main Dishes

(Continued from previous page) Bring the mixture to a boil and then reduce heat to a light simmer. Allow this to simmer for about 20 minutes while tofu is roasting.

Remove the roasted tofu from the oven and with a metal spatula remove tofu from pan without losing too much of the caramelized tofu that is in contact with the pan, Pour into a casserole dish.

Strain out all the ingredients from the mole broth. Place strained ingredients into a blender and slowly add enough of the broth until it has a thick, creamy texture. Add the agave syrup and season with salt and pepper to taste.

Pour the creamy mole sauce over the tofu casserole. Sprinkle 1 tsp. of toasted sesame seeds over the mole and serve.

Recipe by: Brian Espanoza

GLUTEN FREE – PROTEIN RICH

Main Dishes

Vimal's Nut Loaf

Serves 4-6

Ingredients:

1 pound Walnuts. roasted
2 pounds Mushrooms
2 medium Yellow onions
4 cups cooked Brown Rice or Whole oats
4 Tbsp. Oregano
1 4 oz. can Tomato paste
4 Tbsp. Soy sauce or Tamari
6 Large eggs
2 cups Cheddar cheese, shredded
1 cup Parmesan cheese
1 cup Oil
¼ cup Nutritional yeast
1 Tbsp. Salt
1 Tbsp. Pepper
1 Tbsp. Garlic powder

Preparation:

Roast walnuts at 350, until fragrant and lightly browned, then pulse with a food processor. Pulse mushrooms through food processor until chunky, not pureed. Mince onions with food processor. Mix tomato paste and soy sauce/Tamari. Saute onions and mushrooms in a amount of oil until onions are translucent.

In a large separate bowl, mix eggs with the tomato paste and soy sauce/Tamari. Add all the ingredients and thoroughly mix. Lightly oil pan or use parchment paper. Cook at 350 until a tooth pick or small paring knife comes out clean; about 30-45 minutes.

Recipe by: Vimal Dass

Main Dishes

White Beans and Greens

Serves 6-8

Ingredients:
2 ½ cups White beans, dry
2 ¼ bunches Chard
1 1/8 bunches Kale
¾ of Onion
1/3 cup Sesame seeds, roasted, crushed
¼ cup Olive oil
¼ tsp. Thyme
1 Bay leaf

Preparation:
Soak beans overnight. Put beans to boil with bay leaf and thyme. Roast sesame seeds. When beans are cooked, drain and set aside. De-vein and chop greens. Slice onions thin. Saute onions in olive oil over low heat, stirring. When onions are tender and transparent, add greens. When mixed well, sprinkle with roasted, crushed sesame seeds. Gently stir in white beans and drizzle with olive oil.

Recipe by: Vimal Dass

Main Dishes

Yams Roasted with Maple Allspice Butter

Serves 6-8

Ingredients:

½ pound margarine (room temperature)
¼ cup Maple syrup
½ tsp. Salt
½ tsp. Allspice
½ tsp Black pepper
1 yam per person

Preparation:

Mix first 5 ingredients in medium size bowl. Preheat oven to 375. Lightly pierce yams all over with fork. Bake about an hour, until tender when pierced with fork. With knife, cut a cross on top of each yam. Put yams on serving tray. Put Allspice butter in serving bowl.

Recipe by: Marti Waite

Tibetan Foods

Besides being a retreat center for groups of many spiritual denominations, yoga and meditation groups, we are also a Tibetan Buddhist Center.

Momos are Tibetan dumplings filled with stuffing and steamed or boiled. There are thousands of variations on the stuffings; it's fun to experiment and find the flavors that you like the most. The finished dumpling is similar in shape to a Chinese pot sticker. Making momos is best done in the company of others and although making beautiful momos is an art form, ugly momos taste just as good!

One of the highlights of our Medicine Buddha Festival we have each summer is making and serving momos to the 1000 or so guests that come for the Festival.

Many members of the local Tibetan community show up to make the momos. It is a joyous time. And after the momos are made, you can be sure our resident Tibetan monk, Venerable Losang Samten (who was born in Lhasa) makes Thukpa (noodle soup) to serve them.

Although currently we don't serve the Thukpa recipe to our guests, it is so much a part of the Tibetan culture that it had to be included in this *Good Heart Cookbook*.

Chai is often served here after special ceremonies and is always served to the public and friends who attend our New Year's Eve festivities.

Tibetan Foods

Kyabje Lama Zopa Rinpoche's Momo Recipe

Serves 4-6

Ingredients:

4-5 cups flour
1 1/2 cups water
1 16oz. packet frozen chopped spinach
2 bundles fresh mint, minced
2 6oz. packets feta cheese
6 portabella mushrooms
2-4 6oz. pieces fresh mozzarella
1/2 cup grated parmesan
Olive oil

Preparation:

First, prepare the dough.

Place 4 cups of flour in a large bowl. Slowly add water, mixing well, until all the water is absorbed. Add more flour, if needed, to make a smooth ball of dough. Knead the dough for a few minutes; then place in a clean, oiled bowl and cover. Let it sit for at least 15 minutes at room temperature.

Next, prepare the filling.

Rinse spinach in room temperature water and squeeze out all excess moisture with your hands. Allow to drain while you assemble the other ingredients.

Chop feta, mozzarella and mushrooms finely. Or chop together in food processor.

Combine drained spinach, mint, cheeses and mushrooms in a large bowl. Using your hands, mix well. Stir in a generous amount of good olive oil. Cover and refrigerate filling until ready to use. **(Continued on next page)**

Tibetan Foods

Roll out the dough into one long log. Cut in half lengthwise. Roll into thin logs, about one-inch wide. Chop dough into small pieces, about 1/2" long each, forming circles. Flatten circles, then roll with a rolling pin into thin circles.   Cover with a towel to prevent the dough from drying out.

Then, putting the filling in the dough.

Hold one circle in your left hand. Spoon one tablespoon of filling onto the dough. Bring the edges of the dough together and pinch together into a half-moon shape. Alternatively, you can use a pulling and pinching motion to bring the dough over the filling and pinch together at the top. Place assembled momos on a non-stick surface and cover with a slightly damp towel to prevent them from drying out.

Cooking:

Pour two inches of water into the bottom of a steamer and bring to a boil. Add one layer of momos in each section of the steamer. Cover and steam for about 10 minutes. Serve hot with hot sauce and soy sauce.

Alternate Cooking:

Momo Soup: If you don't have a steamer, you can boil momos in a soup: saute some onions and tomatoes in olive oil. Add vegetable broth or water, soy sauce, and any vegetables that sound good. Bring to a boil. Add momos; simmer for about 20 minutes or until momos rise to the top.

Fried Momos: You can also pan fry your momos with some oil on medium heat until the dough is golden brown.

No momo experience is complete without hot sauce for dipping **(See recipe on next page)**

Recipe by: Lama Zopa Rinpoche (Written down with explanations by Venerable Anet, Cynthia "Thea" Crossley and Marti Waite)

VEGAN – GLUTEN FREE

Momo Hot Sauce

Serves 5

Ingredients:
5 ripe Tomatoes, quartered
1 tsp. minced ginger, peeled
3 cloves Garlic, minced
About 3 tsp. Chili powder
About 2 tsp. Hot red chili flakes
2 Tbsp. Vegetable Oil
½ tsp. Tumeric
2 tsp Lemon juice
1 tsp. Tamari
1 tsp. Red wine vinegar
½ onion, minced

Preparation:
Heat a sauce pan over medium heat. Add onion, garlic, chili powder, chili flakes and turmeric. Cook until onions start to soften, about 3 minutes. Add tomato, lemon and Tamari. Bring to a boil, then reduce heat to medium-low, simmer uncovered until tomato is soft and sauce has thickened. Then stir in vinegar.
Add water as needed. Puree mixture. Serve with momos. Taste a small amount then adjust hot peppers and chili flakes to suit your tastes.
Can also substitute chili powder and flakes for deveined, seeded chili peppers. **(see recipe on previous page)**

VEGAN

Tibetan Foods

Thukpa (Tibetan Noodle Soup)

Serves 4

Ingredients:
FOR SOUP
3 cubes Vegetable bullion
4 cloves Garlic, minced
2/3 of Red onion
12 cups Water
2 Tomatoes, chopped
¾ of large Daikon
2 stalks Green onion, chopped
10 cups of spinach – measure before chopping
2 cups Cilantro chopped
FOR DOUGH
3 cups All purpose flour
1 cup Water

Preparation:
Preparing the broth:
Boil 6 cups of water adding 3 bouillon cubes.   Mince
garlic, chop onion. Place garlic and onions in broth and
simmer for about 20 minutes.
Prepare the daikon:
Peel daikon and chop off both ends.   Chop daikon into
thin, narrow strips, as thin as you can make them. Soak the
daikon in water with about 1 teaspoon of salt. Soak for a
few minutes. Rinse well one or more times. The more you
rinse it, the less bitter, salty and radish-tasting the daikon
will taste.
Prepare the other ingredients:
Chop tomatoes into smallish pieces, finely chop the
cilantro, chop green onion, roughly chop spinach in large
pieces. No need to remove stems. **(continued on next page)**

58

Tibetan Foods

Preparing the dough;

In a mixing bowl, place the flour. Slowly add water to the four. Mix to form a smooth ball and then knead for a couple of minutes. The dough does not have to rest after kneading so you can prepare it any time during the process.

Shaping the dough;

First rub the dough ball between your hands to make it into a thick tube of dough. Then pinch the tube into 4-5 inch pieces. Then rub these pieces into long dough ropes and set aside. Use extra water and flour as needed.

Final cooking;

Add another 6 cups of water to the soup and bring to a boil. When soup starts boiling again, add daikon and cook for 2-3 minutes. Now take the dough and break off 1-2 inch pieces and toss them into the soup. Cook for about another 5 minutes. When the noodles are cooked, they will rise to the top. Add spinach, cilantro, green onion and tomato and serve immediately. These final ingredients should not cook through to keep their fresh look.

Recipe printed by permission of "YoWangdu Tibetan Culture
At www.yowangdu.com"

PRECEPT FRIENDLY

Tibetan Foods

Land of Medicine Buddha Chai

Serves 8-10

Ingredients:
6 cups boiling Water
4-5 black tea bags
2 tsp Cardamom (freshly ground)
1 ½ cups Whole milk
1 ½ cups Soy milk
Sugar, agave nectar, or honey till sweet

Preparation:
Boil water. Add the tea bags and cardamom. Boil for one minute. Add milk. Add sugar or agave nectar to taste. Stir and simmer, covered, for 15-20 minutes.

Strain tea through a fine mesh strainer and serve.

Recipe by: "Thea" Cynthia Crossley

Desserts

Squeals of delight arise when the guests look at the menu board and see what's for dessert. We strive to make the desserts a truly perfect end to the day.

It is a rare day when we have much dessert left. And if we do, you can be sure the staff makes short work of it.

We are constantly working to create the healthiest, yummiest desserts we can. And we always try to make sure that we use seasonal, local, organic fruits.

GLUTEN FREE

Desserts

Chocolate Bark

Serves 6-8

Ingredients:
8 oz. Chocolate chips
¼ cup Nuts, chopped
¼ cup Dried Fruit, chopped
¼ tsp. Coarse sea salt

Preparation:
Melt chocolate in double boiler until smooth.   Spray
small cookie sheet with non-stick spray and line with
parchment paper. Pour the melted chocolate into the
cookie sheet and smooth with spatula into an even, thin
layer.   Sprinkle with sea salt, nuts and fruit or other
toppings of your choice.   Refrigerate for about 45
minutes or until completely set and firm. Break into serving
sized pieces and serve with fruit or ice cream or all by
itself.

Recipe by: Karene Percival

GLUTEN FREE

Desserts

Coconut Custard Pie

Makes 2 pies

Ingredients:

FOR CRUST:
1 ½ cups of all purpose flour
1 tsp. Sea salt
3 Tbsp. Apple cider vinegar
4 Tbsp. Cold butter or margarine
FOR FILLING:
2 cups Shredded coconut (unsweetened)
2 tsp. Cornstarch
¾ cup Sugar
2 Whole eggs – 1 egg white
14oz. (1 can) Coconut milk (unsweetened)
Pinch of Sea salt

Preparation:

Mix crust ingredients together in mixing bowl and roll dough into thin crust and place in two 9 inch pie plates. Preheat oven to 350. Combine filling ingredients together in mixing bowl. Pour into pie shells and bake for 35-45 minutes until the fork comes out clean.
Cool in refrigerator for 30 minutes. Serve.

Recipe by: Ruth Nucera

VEGAN – GLUTEN FREE

Desserts

Coconut Tapioca Pudding

Serves 6-8

Ingredients:

3 cups Water
¾ cup Tapioca pearls, dry
1 1/3 cans Coconut milk
½ cup Sugar
¾ tsp. Salt
¾ tsp. Vanilla extract
1 ½ lemons for Lemon zest

Preparation:

In a pot, bring water to a boil. Rinse tapioca, drain and add to the boiling water. Cook gently over medium heat, stirring constantly. When the white tapioca becomes clear and expands, remove from heat; about 8 minutes. Add the coconut milk, sugar and salt. Mix well, and simmer for 5-10 minutes until mixture is hot and sugar dissolves. Do not boil. Keep stirring so it doesn't stick. Turn off heat and mix in vanilla extract. Pour pudding into small bowls or ramekins. Serve alone or with cookies, fruit or chocolate.

Recipe by: Marti Waite

VEGAN – GLUTEN FREE

Desserts

Fruit Crisp

Serves 6-8

Ingredients:

Coconut oil – for saute
1 ¼ quarts Fruit slices – apple or peach or pear, etc.
1 tsp. Cinnamon
2 ½ Tbsp. Agave nectar
1/8 cup Lemon juice
¼ cup Apple juice
¾ Tbsp. Cornstarch
¾ cup Rolled oats
¼ cup Flax seeds
¼ cup Sunflower seeds
¾ cup Walnuts, chopped
½ tsp. Nutmeg
¼ tsp. Cloves
¼ tsp. Salt
¼ cup Coconut oil
2 ½ Tbsp. Maple syrup

Preparation:

Preheat oven to 350. Heat oil in cooking pot. When hot, add fruit, cinnamon, agave, lemon juice, apple juice. Simmer until tender/crisp. Stir in cornstarch, mix well, and turn off heat. The liquid will become syrup almost immediately. Spread mixture into bottom of baking dish. Pulse oats, flax seeds, spices and salt in a food processor with metal blade. In a small pot, heat coconut oil and syrup until smooth. Add to oat mixture and stir until completely combined. Cover fruit with topping. Bake until golden brown; approximately 30 minutes. Serve with whipped cream, if desired.

Recipe by: Marti Waite

GLUTEN FREE

 Desserts

Karene's Chocolate Truffles

Serves: 6-8

Ingredients:

FOR COCONUT BUTTER:
Coconut, shredded unsweetened
FOR FILLING:
5 Tbsp. Yams
2 oz. Chocolate chips
¾ Tbsp. Brown sugar
¼ tsp. Cinnamon
1/8 tsp. Ginger
Pinch of Nutmeg
½ tsp. Vanilla
1/8 tsp. Salt
5 Tbsp. Walnuts
FOR COATING:
¾ Tbsp. Coconut butter
Chocolate chips

Preparation:

Prepare yams:
Place the yams in a saucepan and add cold water to cover. Bring to a boil and simmer for 30 minutes or until done. Drain. Peel yams when cool enough to handle. Cut into 1-inch cubes and put them through a food processor. Put the yams in a saucepan and add remaining ingredients.

(Continued on next page)

Desserts

(Continued from previous page)

Prepare the coconut butter:
To make 1 cup of coconut butter, place 3 cups of unsweetened, shredded coconut in food processor. Mix it for up to 20 minutes, scraping down the sides every few minutes until mixture becomes very smooth and creamy. Set aside.
Prepare filling:
Chop walnuts. Using a double boiler, melt chocolate, stirring continuously. Add coconut butter and sugar. Mix thoroughly. Set aside to cool, slightly. Add pureed yams, cinnamon, ginger, nutmeg, vanilla and salt to melted chocolate and mix well. Fold in nuts.   Cover and refrigerate for 30-60 minutes. Form mixture into 1 inch balls.   Place on parchment lined baking sheet and freeze for at least 1 hour until hardened.
For coating:
Using a double boiler, melt remaining chocolate with coconut butter.   Stir until smooth. Remove from heat and dip each truffle in chocolate.   Before serving, refrigerate for about 10 minutes.

Recipe by: Karene Percival

PRECEPT FRIENDLY

Desserts

Strawberry Shortcake

Serves 6-8

Ingredients:
1 ½ quarts Fresh Strawberries
½ cup Sugar
2 ½ cups All purpose flour
3 ½ tsp. Baking powder
1 tsp. Salt
6 Tbsp. Coconut oil
1 ¼ cup Milk

Preparation:
Wash berries.   Drain well.   Remove stems and hulls.
Add sugar and let stand at room temperature for an
hour. Heat oven to 450.   Measure flour by dip-level-pour
method. Stir flour, sugar baking powder and salt in a
bowl.   Cut in coconut oil.   Stir in milk until just blended.
Spread into greased pan. Bake around 20 minutes.
When done, cut into squares.   Serve with bowls of
sugared strawberries and whipped cream.

Recipe By: Karene Percival

Extras

As any good cook will tell you, there are many little details and extras that go into creating a good meal.

We've included just a few of them here.

Hope they bring you as much joy eating them as they do in making them.

From our good heart to yours, enjoy!

VEGAN – GLUTEN FREE

Extras

Hummus Veggie Wrap

Serves 6-8

Ingredients:
Hummus
Cucumber, julienned '
Red pepper, julienned
Cabbage, shredded
Carrot, shredded
6-8 Tortillas

Preparation:
Prepare or purchase your favorite hummus. Best kind is one with mild garlic and/or mild lemon.   Prepare peanut sauce.   Arrange ingredients on the tortilla. Add peanut sauce.   Roll and serve.

Recipe by: Vimal Dass

VEGAN – GLUTEN FREE

Extras

Salsa Fresca

Serves 6-8

Ingredients:
½ Onion, cut into large chunks
2 Garlic cloves, peeled
2 Jalapeno pepper
1 bunch Cilantro
2 Lemons, juiced
2 small cans Tomatoes, drained
Salt and Pepper – to tasted

Preparation:
Place all ingredients in the food processor or blender.
Pulse first Jalapeno, cilantro, onion and garlic.   Then add
the tomatoes.   Pulse again, leaving it chunky.   Add lemon
juice and salt and pour into a bowl.   Serve with chips or as
a garnish.

Recipe by: Vimal Dass

Extras

Savory Pesto Popcorn

Serves 6

Ingredients:
½ cup Pop popcorn
1 cup Walnuts, roasted
1 cup fresh Basil
¼ cup Parmesan cheese
½ tsp. Salt
4 cloves Garlic
¼ cup Olive oil

Preparation:
FOR PESTO: Roast walnuts at 350 - until lightly toasted and fragrant. Then cool. In a food processor or blender add cooled walnuts, basil, garlic and salt. Pulse to mix thoroughly. Once mixed, add all the parmesan and half the oil. Run for 1 minute. Add the rest of the oil slowly until reaching desired consistency. FOR POPCORN: Pop the popcorn. Mix pesto thoroughly with popcorn. Serve and enjoy.

Recipe by: Vimal Dass

VEGAN – PROTEIN RICH

Spanish Romesco Sauce

Serves 4-6

Ingredients:
4 Roma (plum) tomatoes, halved
1 large Red bell pepper, quartered
7 cloves Garlic
1/3 cup and 1 Tbsp. Olive oil.
Salt to taste
2 large slices old sourdough bread (any kind of simple bread)
¼ cup and 2 tsps. Whole Almonds, toasted
¼ cup and 2 tsps. Red wine vinegar
¼ tsp. Spanish paprika
Pinch crushed Red pepper flakes, or to taste

Preparation:
Preheat oven to 425. Place the tomatoes, bell pepper and garlic cloves into an oiled casserole (glass or ceramic is fine). Brush the vegetables with some of the olive oil, then sprinkle with salt. Bake in preheated oven until the garlic has turned golden brown, 25-35 minutes. Remove from oven, and allow to cool for 10 minutes. Meanwhile, fry the bread slices on a well oiled pan until golden brown on both sides. Remove and allow to cool.
Scrape the vegetables and any juices from the pan and into a food processor or blender. Break the bread into pieces and add to the food processor along with the toasted almonds, vinegar, paprika, and red pepper flakes. Puree until finely ground. Drizzle remaining olive oil. Season with additional salt if necessary.

Recipe by: Brian Espanoza

VEGAN – PROTEIN FRIENDLY

Tofu Crumble

Serves 6-8

Ingredients:
1 pound extra firm Tofu
2 Tbsp. Nutritional Yeast
2 Tbsp. Tamari
1 Tbsp. Garlic powder
½ tsp. dried Savory
4 Tbsp. Olive oil

Preparation:
Preheat oven to 400. Press tofu for at least 30 minutes to rid it of as much water as possible. Well oil a cookie sheet. With your hands, rough crumble tofu into a mixing bowl making sure not to break it up smaller than grape sized pieces. Toss thoroughly with seasonings and oil.
Bake at 400 degrees on well oiled sheet for about 30 minutes or until firm. At least once during baking, remove from oven and stir to make sure all sides toast evenly.
NOTE: Additional seasonings may be added to complement various dishes. For example for Asian flavor, omit Nutritional yeast and add ginger powder.
Serve as a topping, taco filling or as a side for a salad bar.

Recipe by: Brian Espanoza

Cooking with Bodhichitta Mindfulness

by Gelongma Losang Drimay

Lama Zopa Rinpoche emphasizes that we should not waste any opportunity for Dharma practice. We can turn even our ordinary everyday activities into Dharma—the causes for enlightenment—by combining them with certain positive thoughts. Bodhichitta is the mind of a bodhisattva having the intent to become a Buddha for the sake of all sentient beings. Bodhichitta mindfulness consists of thoughts of benefiting others, specifically by leading them out of suffering and delusion and leading them to enlightenment. In that process, there are many things to be purified and other things to be actualized. Rinpoche has done some cooking demonstrations explaining how to think when we do each part of the preparation, but once you get the idea you can come up with some of your own slogans. Here are some examples of Rinpoche's bodhichitta mindfulness sayings.

Begin your cooking with a bodhichitta motivation: "By this action of cooking, I am leading all sentient beings to enlightenment. May I cherish all sentient beings immediately and free them from every suffering. May all their suffering come onto the 'I' and may they receive all the happiness."

Then combine each step with a related mindfulness, like this:

While peeling vegetables, think, "I am removing sentient beings' delusions."

While shredding vegetables, think, "I am destroying self-cherishing thought."

While adding flour to a broth, think, "I am adding realizations."

While stirring a mixture (such as the filling for momos), think, "I am taming sentient beings' minds."

While rolling out dough (such as for pies), think, "I am eliminating mistaken thoughts toward the guru."

While pinching the dough together (such as the momo wrapper around the filling), think, "I am gathering together the five paths and the ten bhumis (the levels of realization on the way to Buddhahood)."

Let your good heart be your guide.

Eating with Bodhichitta Mindfulness

As we are a Tibetan Buddhist Retreat center we thought it would be nice to include these food offering prayers in English and with Tibetan phonetics for those who are so inclined.

Sometimes it can be very difficult to eat mindfully, especially when the food is delicious. Starting a meal with a food offering prayer can be a good way to remind us to eat more mindfully. Even if we do loose our mindfulness after a couple of bites, it is for us still meaningful to think of the Guru, Buddha, Dharma, and Sangha before we eat.

Before you begin to eat, you could take a minute to look at your food and reflect on how many people worked so that you can have this meal. The farmers, people in the stores, people who prepared your food, etc.

OM AH HUM - *(Recite three times. This represents the enlightened body speech and mind of the Buddhas and our own potential.)*

TÖN PA LA ME SANG GYÄ RIN PO CHHE
To the supreme teacher, the precious Buddha,
KYAB PA LA ME DAM CHHÖ RIN PO CHHE
To the supreme refuge, the precious Dharma,
DREN PA LA ME GE DÜN RIN PO CHHE
To the supreme guides, the precious Sangha,
KYAB NÄ KÖN CHHOG SUM LA CHHÖ PA BÜL
To the Triple Gem, the objects of refuge, I make offering.

LA MA SANG GYÄ LA MA CHHÖ
The Guru is Buddha, the Guru is Dharma,
DE ZHIN LA MA GE DÜN TE
The Guru is Sangha also.
KÜN GYI JE PO LA MA TE
The Guru is the creator of all (happiness).
LA MA NAM LA CHHÖ PAR BÜL
To all gurus, I make this offering.

Mahayana Precepts Diet

In the Buddhist Mahayana tradition, to help increase our compassion for all sentient beings, there are practices where the practitioner takes specific vows for a 24 hour period. This practice is suitable for members of the monastic community as well as lay people.

"Upon taking the Eight Mahayana Precepts, one must avoid black foods, such as meat, eggs, radishes, garlic and onions, and eat food of the three white substances before noon, in one sitting, and not get up to take a second helping. One must then abandon eating food at the wrong time—from noon that day until sunrise the next." - from *Direct and Unmistaken Method*, By Kyabje Lama Zopa Rinpoche

Some monastics (monks and nuns) choose to keep the precept diet all the time. Some lay Buddhist practitioners also decide to keep this diet to support their spiritual practice. Still others may decide observe the precepts only on holy days or before taking an empowement. Some Buddhists are vegetarian, others are not.

If you are interested in learning more about taking the Eight Mahayana Precepts visit (http://www.fpmt.org/prayers/8precepts.php). Please note that the first time one takes the precepts, it is taken from a master who holds the lineage. Thereafter, one can do the ceremony before a Buddha image by regarding it as the actual Buddha.

About Land of Medicine Buddha

Land of Medicine Buddha is a green certified, pet friendly, non-profit retreat center located in Santa Cruz County. We offer Buddhist classes and retreats, space for personal retreats, as well as rental facilities for private groups to hold their own spiritual workshops, conferences, and trainings.

The goal of our Center, based on the principles taught by Shakyamuni Buddha and promoted worldwide by His Holiness Dalai Lama, is to nurture healing and the development of a good heart, which includes the cultivation of compassion and loving kindness. As such, the center aspires to teach principles for living that are universally applicable.

We have many inspiring things to see on our land including two beautiful meditation halls which house a sand mandala, inspirational life size statues, paintings of Buddhas and deities. They provide a harmonious setting where we offer transformational classes, retreats and rituals relating to the study and integration of Buddhist practices in our daily life. We also perform daily water bowl offerings and Medicine Buddha pujas.

In addition, we are stewards of 108 acres of redwood forest and a peaceful meadow for hiking and meditation; provide genuine customer service performed by a team dedicated to your happiness; have simple and comfortable rooms with private bathrooms; (and of course) serve delicious vegetarian cuisine prepared fresh daily and cooked with love by a team of professional chefs.

Land of Medicine Buddha was established in 1983 by two

Tibetan Buddhist masters, Lama Thubten Yeshe and Kyabje Lama Zopa Rinpoche. It was their vision for Land of Medicine Buddha to be a place of ultimate healing.

We're affiliated with FPMT, Foundation for the Preservation of the Mahayana Tradition, an international organization of 147 Centers and social projects worldwide.

Our center is proud to help support the preservation of the Tibetan culture. We feel blessed to be helping keep alive amazing Tibetan art forms, as is seen in our Wish Fulfilling Temple, Gompa, Statues, Stupas and Prayer Wheels.

We continue to reach out to the local community in a variety of ways including our annual festivals.

Sustainability and non-harming is important to us and we are certified "green" with the Monterey Bay Green Business Program. Our center is engaged in many inspiring projects including upgrading of facilities to be more environmentally conscious, improving accessibility to our buildings, and building a magnificent stupa for world peace.

Please visit our website at:
www.landofmedicinebuddha.org

Please visit our retreat center at:
Land of Medicine Buddha
5800 Prescott Road
Soquel CA 95073 -   USA
(831) 462-8383

Made in the USA
Charleston, SC
23 January 2016